Montréal

Photography by
Larry Fisher

Irving Weisdorf & Co. Ltd.

Montreal, an island in the St. Lawrence River, is a very beautiful and unique North American city — one that is enjoyed by millions of visitors and tourist each year.

Montreal, an island, takes its name from the "Royal Mountain," a scenic backdrop to the downtown core. With the mountain at its back and the stately St. Lawrence River around its shores, Montreal, the second-largest of Canada's cities, is one of the country's most scenic urban centres. A major draw for tourists, it attracts over nine million visitors per year.

One of the country's oldest cities (it celebrated its 350th anniversary in 1992), metropolitan Montreal is also the second-largest French-speaking metropolis in the world, home to over 3.2 million people. Many other languages are spoken here too, because immigrants have come from every corner of the world, making Montreal a vibrant, multicultural community.

The cultural diversity of the population and the city's fascinating history — a history which goes back to the native settlement of Hochelaga and the fur-trading days of the 17th century — have influenced the look of the city's buildings, whose architecture is a rich blend of the old and the new.

Montreal's architecture and its lively, fashionable people have helped to put it on the international map. The city has won accolades around the world especially since hosting two major events — EXPO '67 and in 1976, the Olympic Games. The World Fair and the Olympic Games were followed by a myriad of international festivals —

among them the acclaimed Jazz Festival, Juste Pour Rire/Just For Laughs (a bilingual comedy fest) and the Benson & Hedges Inc. International Fireworks Competition — colourful celebrations which have become annual fixtures in Montreal's social calendar.

There's more to Montreal than festivals, however. The city has many historic sites and landmarks and its museums rank among the best in North America. The Montreal Museum of Fine Arts, the Museum of Contemporary Art and the Pointe-à-Callière Museum of Archeology and History are not just a showcase for the culture and history of Quebec and Canada, but stunning buildings which are themselves, major drawing cards.

The contrast between the old and new is very pronounced. You'll find chic bistros housed in 18th-century rowhouses; Victorian homes nestled under office towers of concrete and steel and a people whose personalities reveal a laid-back, European flair, underneath a hard-working North American veneer. These unexpected contrasts form a seductive blend that makes Montreal one of the most fascinating places in North America.

(opposite page) Montreal's skyline, so beautiful by night, shows some of the charm and character the city has to offer.

HISTORY

Montreal's beginnings were not entirely peaceful. European settlement began in 1642, with the arrival of Paul de Chomedey de Maisonneuve (one of Montreal's east-west thoroughfares carries his name). He was charged with the task of founding a mission — Ville-Marie — to "convert" the native Iroquois, who, understandably, resisted this interference in their traditional way of life. There were numerous skirmishes between the Indians and the newly-arrived settlers, especially over who should control the lucrative fur trade.

Despite the difficulties, a European settlement started to take root only one year later. Maisonneuve succeeded in establishing a fort, a hospital, a chapel and housing for over 70 people. Although he disappeared from Montreal's history (in 1665 he was recalled to France), Ville-Marie continued to grow and flourish.

Quebec City took its place as the administrative centre of New France and the principal port, but Montreal quickly became the centre of the interior — the gateway to the vast wilderness that held untold riches in the form of furs. A population of coureurs de bois, voyageurs and famous explorers made Montreal their base and from here they fanned out into the hinterland.

Many of the most famous names in North American history were these early Montreal adventurers — Cavalier de Lasalle, who claimed Louisiana for Louis XIV; Lamothe Cadillac, who founded Detroit and La Vérendrye who pushed his way westwards as far as the Rocky Mountains.

The fur trade continued to be the economic mainstay of Montreal after the British gained control of Quebec in 1760. The city surrendered a year after the Battle of the Plains of Abraham. Scottish merchants replaced the francophone entrepreneurs and men such as Alexander Mackenzie, the Frobisher brothers, Simon McTavish and William McGillivray, amassed huge fortunes. This was the era of the great fur trading cartels like the North West Company and the Hudson's Bay Company, still in business today.

In the early 1800s, there was an influx of immigrants from Britain and by 1844, Montreal had overtaken Quebec City as the most important metropolis in French-speaking Canada. The mid-19th century was a period of great expansion. The mercantile classes, now primarily British in origin and English-speaking rather than French, founded important commercial enterprises, largely involved in the import and export trade.

Wilfred Laurier.

The Bank of Montreal, built in 1847, is Montreal's oldest bank building. This building is not only a great place to see, both inside and out, but also an informative place to visit — a small banking museum allows visitors to see how banking was in days gone by.

Robert Burns.

The Montreal History Centre is housed in the old Central Fire Station, built in 1903. The Centre thrills history buffs and intrigues both residents and tourists as it traces the history of the city from its first settlers in 1642 to the present day.

Bonsecours Market, erected in 1845 in Old Montreal, is a beautiful neoclassic building and an architectural pleasure. Its brilliant dome and handsome facade add yet more charm to the city.

Dominion Square.

By the turn of the 20th century, Montreal was the preeminent metropolis in the entire country, not just the province of Quebec. Further immigration and new developments in the transportation and distribution network — namely building the transcontinental railway and deepening the St. Lawrence River between Montreal and Quebec City — led to Montreal becoming a major manufacturing hub, as well as a centre of trade.

The past 30 years has seen a decline in Montreal's position as a commercial centre. In the 1970s, economic power and expertise shifted to Toronto, partly due to the resurgence of Quebec nationalism which prompted major corporations to move their offices and plants to a less volatile place, and partly because of a natural cycle in the economic life of the country. Interestingly, though Toronto is considered the economic "engine" of Canada, it may be overtaken in turn by Vancouver, whose surging economy reflects its strong trading links to the buoyant Pacific Rim.

Montreal will, no doubt, go through many more cycles, both economic and political, during the next few decades but as in the past, its vibrant and unique personality will leave its mark on the world.

Montreal's City Hall (right) is beautiful and historic both inside and out. Built between 1872 and 1878, this structure was almost lost to a terrible fire in 1922. The exterior walls survived and the rest, plus an additional floor, was rebuilt and opened again in 1926.

Montreal is an easy city to get around, but don't forget it is strictly prohibited to make a right on a red light in the province of Quebec. Most of the road signs are in both English and French but there are some that are only French. If you are not driving on the well-developed highways and streets there are many options — from walking to trains, buses and tours by caleche, boat or plane.

The unique Olympic Stadium, built for the 1976 Olympics, is a well known landmark in Montreal and one that is recognized in many city scenes.

MOUNT ROYAL PARK

Mount Royal is, for Montrealers, as important a landmark as Rio de Janeiro's Sugarloaf Mountain, Sydney's Opera House or Edinburgh's imposing castle. In the psyche of urbanites, the mountain is an almost sacred place, a 500-acre green space of old trees and manicured walkways in the middle of the throbbing city.

The park is a favourite gathering place for Montrealers who come here to walk, cycle, jog, picnic, skate and cross country ski. It was designed by Frederick Law Olmsted, the American landscape architect who also laid out New York's Central Park. Appointed the first commissioner of Yosemite National Park in California, Olmsted was one of the first landscapers to preserve the natural look of the land (in the 19th century, the tendency was to "tame" the wilderness) — something that he has certainly achieved in the layout of Mount Royal Park.

Mount Royal was named by French explorer Jacques Cartier, who claimed Quebec for his king, Francis I. On his second expedition to New France, in 1535, he climbed the 232-metre peak. The mountain's natural beauty continues to attract visitors. **Beaver Lake**, which lies within the park's grounds, is a favourite gathering place.

The front terrace of the Mount Royal chalet lookout is a popular spot for city residents as well as tourists. This location provides a wonderful view. The chalet itself has a historical exhibit and hosts many receptions and concerts.

(above) Beaver Lake, in Mount Royal Park, is a great spot for sunbathing, boating and picnicking in the summer months and an equally great spot for skating and skiing in the winter.

(left) The George-Etienne Cartier statue is a popular spot, especially on Sundays when hundreds of people gather around the statue to listen to improvised music.

(below) The sight of the cross on Mount Royal is a familiar one in Montreal. This illuminated cross, erected in 1924, symbolizes the wooden cross that Maisonneuve is said to have erected on this spot in 1642.

From a lookout point near the top, visitors can see the city and the St. Lawrence River, spread like a giant map at Mount Royal's feet. An interpretation centre explains the ecology of the park. At the peak is a striking cross, erected in 1924 to commemorate a promise made by Paul de Chomedey de Maisonneuve, the founder of Montreal. Grateful that the fledgling French colony, then called Ville-Marie, had survived a devastating flood, he erected a wooden cross on January 6, 1642. The modern monument, which is 30 metres high, is illuminated at night and can be seen from several kilometres away.

The best view of Montreal is from 232 metres above sea level on Mount Royal. What a breath-taking spot to view the city.

This grand Italian Renaissance-style basilica was built in 1966 by Montreal's Catholics in honour of St. Joseph, patron saint of Canada, and in memory of Brother André. A statue of St. Joseph meets those who arrive to see the magnificent shrine named for him. The shrine, at 263 metres, is the highest point in Montreal.

At the south eastern end of Mount Royal Park, is **St. Joseph's Oratory**, one of North America's most visited shrines. It attracts over two million pilgrims annually, who come to pay homage to the father of Jesus. The basilica, whose copper dome is the second-largest in the world after St. Peter's in Rome, was begun in 1942 and completed several years later. The shrine houses the chapel of the Blessed Sacrament and a museum dedicated to the life of Brother André, a priest who was elevated to sainthood by the Vatican, in 1982.

On the other side of the mountain are what remains of some of the huge homes built by Montreal's elite merchant class in the mid-1800s. Wealthy francophones gravitated towards Outrement — an area that is today favoured by trendy media types and a large community of Orthodox Hassidic Jews. Westmount, with its elegant homes and well-tended gardens, was the bastion of wealthy anglophone Montrealers. Nowadays, the community is mixed.

St. Joseph's Oratory is imposing by night with its beautiful lighting and impressive, shining dome.

OLD MONTREAL

In colonial times, military ceremonies were held in **Place d'Armes**. A statue of Montreal's founder, **Paul de Chomedey de Maisonneuve**, stands guard in the middle of the square. When French colonists arrived in 1642, they quickly turned Montreal (Ville-Marie) into the fur trading capital of North America. In the 18th and 19th centuries, Montreal became Canada's leading industrial centre — an era that is echoed in the architecture of many of its commercial buildings. The imposing **Bank of Montreal** (1847) with its opulent, marble-pillared interior, is typical of the city's prosperous Victorian period.

Driving around Old Montreal in a horse-drawn caleche is a relaxing way to explore the oldest and one of the most interesting parts of town. Let your mind drift back in time while your driver explains the history and enjoy looking at some of Quebec's most beautiful churches and public buildings.

(below) Place d'Armes is a favourite spot with tourists. Surrounded by some of the oldest buildings in the city, the square where Maissoneuve and his fellow founders stand is the perfect spot to see and feel the beauty and history of Old Montreal.

(above) In the centre of Place d'Armes is a monument to the founder of Montreal, Paul de Chomedey de Maisonneuve (1612-1676). Maisonneuve remained in the area for 23 years after winning a mortal combat with the Iroquois chief. The site of the monument marks the spot where the Iroquois were defeated by the settlers. The monument reads: "You are the buckwheat seed which will grow and multiply and spread throughout the country."

Facing Place d'Armes is the classic Bank of Montreal — Montreal's oldest bank building. Its beautiful dome and elegant facade are a treat to see, while its handsome columns add even more historical flavour.

The inside of the Bank of Montreal, renovated from 1901 to 1905, is breathtaking. There's much to admire, including the enormous and imposing columns of syenite granite.

The Saint-Sulpice Seminary, constructed in 1683, is the oldest structure in Montreal. Of particular interest is the 1701 clock, an outstanding example of New France architecture. Another architectural gem is the **Old Court House**, built in the neo-classical style of the mid-19th century. Civil cases tried under the Quebec Civil Code, which is based Napoleonic Law, were once heard here.

The heart of Old Montreal is **Place Jacques Cartier**, a lively square flanked by flower beds and sidewalk cafés. Street performers and strolling musicians entertain the diners. At the far end of the square is Nelson's Column, dedicated to the hero of Trafalgar, and the handsome City Hall, built in Second Empire style in the late 19th century. Near the south west corner of the square is **rue Saint-Amable**, a gathering place for artists who sell everything from pocket-size sketches to large, colourful canvases.

Most of the Old Courthouse was built in 1856 except for the dome and third floor which were added on 35 years after. This old building certainly served its purpose since it heard the city's civil cases until the new courthouse, the Palais de Justice, was built next door in 1978. The Old Courthouse now serves as a home to civic departments of the City of Montreal.

The Sulpician Seminary, which faces Place d'Armes, is the oldest building in Montreal and the walls that surround it are just as old. This structure was built by the Sulpician priests in 1658, one year after they arrived in Ville-Marie. Although the seminary is not open to visitors, just seeing it from outside offers a wonderful slice of history — the clock on the facade, for example, dates back to 1701 and moves from instruments made almost entirely of wood.

Adding to the charm and atmosphere of Old Montreal, street artists are popular for both their art and entertainment value.

Place Jacques Cartier, which was originally opened as a market- place back in 1804, is now the most popular Old City square. Tourists and residents both flock to this enchanting place to feel and experience its cobble stone streets, outdoor cafes, vendors and historic buildings — it's like travelling back 200 years in time. The caleches departing from the square, for horse- drawn tours of Old Montreal, add yet another element to the old-fashioned charm of this area.

On rue Saint Paul are the **Bonsecours Market** and **Notre-Dame-de-Bonsecours Chapel**, commonly known as the "Sailors Church". The latter, built in 1773 at the instigation of Marguerite Bourgeoys, Montreal's first teacher, gets its name from the models of ships suspended from the ceiling inside. They were hung there by sailors and their families in thanks to the Virgin Mary for safe passages at sea. At the back of the church is a museum dedicated to the saintly Marguerite Bourgeoys.

Bonsecours Market, constructed in neo-classical style in the middle of the 19th century, served for a short time as the federal government headquarters, after the parliament buildings in Ottawa burned down. Bonsecours was a public trading place for almost a century and now serves as an exhibition hall.

Notre-Dame-de-Bonsecours chapel is called the "Sailors' Church" because of the wooden ship models hanging inside which the sailors gave to the church as thanks for being saved at sea. There is a museum in the basement of this church which tells the story of the woman, Marguerite Bourgeoys, who founded the church and a nuns' order called the Congregation of Notre-Dame. This nun and teacher was made a saint in 1982. The tower of the old church is a great place for a view of Old Montreal.

(right) Rue Saint Paul has much to see and do. The dome of the Bonsecours market shines brilliantly as people make their way through shops and to restaurants.

The beauty and setting of Bonsecours Market make it worth visiting even if there is nothing going on in the building. It is used today, for exhibition space as it was for the five month long celebration of Montreal's 350th birthday. In the past it was used as a market place of course, a city hall and for government offices. Unofficially it served as a landmark, since at one time the distinct silver dome could be seen from anywhere in the city and those at sea could rely on it to guide them into the harbour.

(above) The IMAX Theatre in the Old Port offers a different kind of Old Montreal experience. This attraction is fun for the whole family, with larger-than-life views of topics on a seven-storey screen.

(right) This monument to Lord Horatio Nelson, hero of Trafalgar, was erected in 1809 and can be found at the north end of Place Jacques Cartier. He certainly adds to the historic and old-fashioned atmosphere of his surroundings.

(left) Although it was built in 1878, Montreal's City Hall is one of the most modern structures in Old Montreal. It is a beautiful back drop to many Old Montreal scenes.

Notre Dame houses one of the largest organs in the world. The east tower encases a 10-bell carillon. The west tower holds a monster bell weighing 11,240 kilograms, a distinctive sound when calling the faithful to prayer. The basilica is a mecca for music lovers who come to listen to the many concerts staged in the church. Notre Dame's wooden interior creates outstanding acoustics. Italian tenor, Luciano Pavarotti, recorded his popular Christmas concert here. The Montreal Symphony Orchestra (MSO) which has many albums and CDs to its credit, has also recorded in the basilica. Every winter, the MSO performs Handel's "Messiah" to a packed house.

The **Montreal History Centre**, which used to be a fire station, gives a good overview of the city's past — from its early beginnings in the 17th century, through its industrial era, to the present. The exhibits take visitors back in time in a colourful and interesting way. In one room they can board an old streetcar. In another, they stand in a 1940s living room, listening to a radio broadcast of "Hockey Night in Canada," a sound steeped in nostalgia for those old enough to remember when this program was the social highlight of the week.

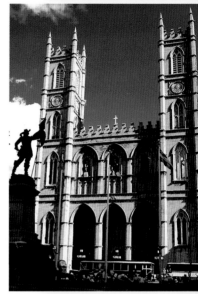

The beautiful and magnificent Notre-Dame Basilica was designed by American architect James O'Donnell in 1829. Local legend says he was so inspired by his creation that upon finishing it he converted to Catholicism. This story may be true, since he is one of the few people buried here. The basilica faces Place d'Armes where Maisonneuve watches over the comings and goings of this famous structure.

(right) The breathtaking interior of the Notre-Dame Basilica is magnificent with rich colours and striking design. The organ is one of the largest in the world and the main pulpit is hand carved. This amazing place is even more of a sight when it is full with the 3,500 worshippers it is capable of holding.

The Montreal History Centre, in Place d'Youville, is a historical building in itself. It was built in 1903 as the city's Central Fire Station. The displays, exhibits and videos inside the centre offer a genuine blast to the past. Every aspect of Montreal's history is covered from its founding in 1642 to the present day.

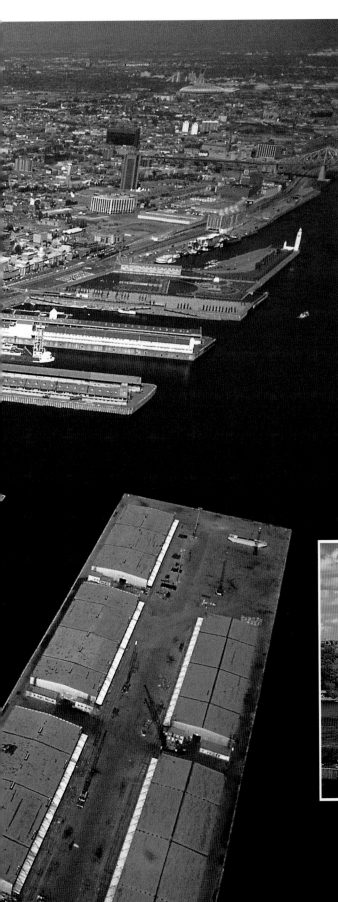

The Montreal History Centre is a stone's throw from the "**Vieux Port**" (Old Port), also part of Old Montreal. What makes the waterfront so interesting is that while just over two kilometres has been turned into a tourist attraction, this is still very much a working port, with 100 berths and five container terminals spread along 25 kilometres of shoreline. Cargoes of minerals, forest products and automobile parts are shipped out through Montreal's port.

About 40 commercial shipping lines use the port, as well as a large number of cruise companies and a range of vessels — from glass topped sightseeing boats, to luxurious "floating hotels" — provide a colourful backdrop to the other attractions at the Vieux Port. Visit the **Clock Tower**, EXPOTEC (an interactive exhibition explaining how electricity works) and the IMAX movie theatre with its seven-storey-high screen. From the Clock Tower, see a panoramic view over the Vieux Port, nearby Bassin Bonsecours and the St. Lawrence River.

The Clock Tower is a familiar part of the skyline when out on the St. Lawrence River looking into Montreal's Old Port. Boat tours leave from this landmark spot and the tower is also a popular spot to catch an overall view of Old Port and the St. Lawrence River.

The Pavilion Bassin du Bonsecours is a wonderful place for a wonderful view of both Montreal and the St. Lawrence River.

ON THE WATER

The Vieux Port is only one of many attractions on the St. Lawrence River. The island of Montreal is linked to the south shore by the Jacques Cartier and Champlain bridges (named for the two great explorers of New France) and the Victoria Bridge (named after Queen you-know-who).

Between the Victoria and Jacques Cartier bridges lie two islands — Ile Sainte-Hélène and Ile Notre-Dame to the south — both of which offer a myriad of things to enjoy while in Montreal. Parc des Iles (as the islands are collectively known), was a venue for the millions of visitors who came to enjoy EXPO '67 and they've been popular places of entertainment ever since.

Habitat '67, a futuristic housing complex at Cité du Havre, which looks like a pile of giant concrete building bricks set at odd angles, also dates back to the 1967 World's Fair. Over 100 apartments are housed in the 345 modules that make up the innovative housing scheme. Designed by renowned Israeli-Canadian architect Moshe Safdie, Habitat was well ahead of its time.

Ile Sainte-Hélène was named by Samuel de Champlain in 1611, in honour of his wife, Hélène Broulé. Today the park is dominated by a giant geodesic dome, the U.S. pavilion during EXPO '67. Another remnant of the World's Fair is 'Man' a large sculpture by Alexander Calder, the American artist known for his abstract, modernistic stabiles.

Habitat '67 was built as a futuristic housing complex for the World's Fair — it is still spoken of today as looking futuristic. It features over 100 apartments in the 345 modules.

(right) Jacques Cartier Bridge provides a different and scenic way to see Montreal as it passes over Ile Ste-Helene.

Pleasure boats docked at Montreal's harbour add charm to the already graceful scene of the city.

Montrealers and their families head for **La Ronde**, an amusement park with many spine-tingling rides, at the northern tip of the island. Open only during the summer, the amusement park, which attracts over one million visitors annually, is also the venue for the **Benson & Hedges International Fireworks Competition**. The fireworks competition runs from mid-June to mid-July and it features spectacular, themed displays of light and sound, representing different countries and cultures.

Ile Notre-Dame, to the south of Ile Saint-Hélène, is man-made and was created especially for EXPO '67. Like its neighbour, much of it is parkland, landscaped with canals and manicured, colourful flower beds, the legacy of Floralies Internationales, a floral competition held in 1980.

In the summer, vacationers flock to the beach (also man-made) and the outdoor theatre. Circling Ile Notre-Dame is

La Ronde, Montreal's well-known amusement park, is located on Ile Ste-Helene and features 35 rides plus lots of family entertainment and fun.

The Montreal Casino, the province's first casino, is a hot spot with both tourists and residents. It was opened, in 1993, in the modern French Pavilion from Expo '67. There is enough room and entertainment for 5,300 people, daily from 11 a.m. to 3 a.m.

the Gilles-Villeneuve racing track, the circuit for Montreal's annual Formula I Grand Prix. In early February, the island is crowded with visitors once more, during the Fêtes des Neiges, a celebration of the winter season.

Year round, tourists and locals alike flock to the **Montreal Casino**, housed in a building which served as the French pavilion during EXPO '67. Since opening its doors in October 1993, the casino, which looks like a giant flying saucer surrounded by spikes, has been a resounding success, attracting over four million visitors annually. They come to try their luck at the 88 gaming tables (there's everything from Blackjack to Keno) and 1,700 slot machines, or to enjoy the glamorous ambience of Nuances, an elegant restaurant on the fifth floor, where high-rollers dine in cocktail dresses and tuxedos.

One of the largest attractions at La Ronde each year is the Benson & Hedges International Fireworks Competition. The displays are held at 10 p.m., on Saturdays in June and Sundays in July.

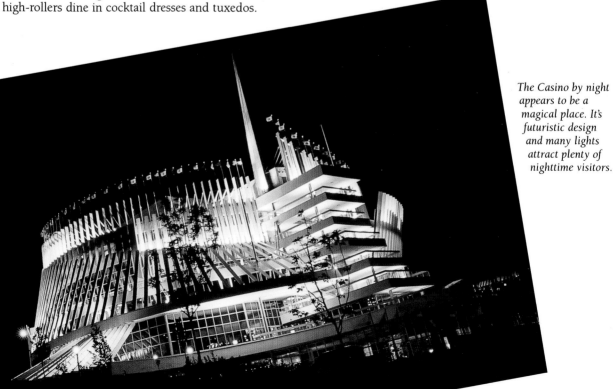

The Casino by night appears to be a magical place. It's futuristic design and many lights attract plenty of nighttime visitors.

ATTRACTIONS

One of Montreal's prime attractions is the **Botanical Garden** and Insectarium, in the heart of the city.

Here, Mother Nature, not man, rules supreme. Growing in colourful profusion in 10 greenhouses and 30 manicured gardens, are over 26,000 species of plants and shrubs from around the world.

The Botanical Garden, which is considered to be one of the best in the world, is not only a tourist attraction, but an important research centre. It's affiliated with the University of Montreal's Plant Biology Research Institute which is located on the grounds.

The entire park is landscaped with walkways, rockeries, waterfalls and reflecting pools — a natural backdrop which makes walking here a pleasure. Of all the displays, the **Rose Garden** is perhaps the most impressive. Thousands of dazzling blooms in every shade of the rainbow, surround visitors in a swath of colour, assaulting the senses at every turn. Sailing amid a sea of roses, at the southern entrance of the botanical garden, is a bronze statue of a lion, a gift to Montreal from the City of Lyon, France.

Montreal's beautiful and famous Botanical Garden spreads across 180 acres of land. Visitors to the garden can expect to see an amazing 26,000 plant types in over 30 special gardens. Displays change year round making it a place to visit over and over again.

Roses bloom in the International Rose Garden from mid-June until the frost arrives. This spot is a favourite among visitors.

(right) A picturesque waterfall is one of the many naturally beautiful sights to see at Montreal's Botanical Garden.

One of the newest additions to the Botanical Garden is the **Insectarium**, which was opened in 1990. Over a quarter of a million insects, everything from horrific looking tarantulas to beautifully coloured butterflies, are on show here.

Teaching visitors about the natural wonders of the world is the idea behind the **Biodome**, a cross between an educational establishment, a zoo, an aquarium and a museum. The Biodome, which is situated across the street from the Botanical Garden and is part of the Olympic Park complex (it was used for cycling events during the 1976 Olympic Games), is a "world" in miniature, representing four environments — the St. Lawrence Marine Ecosystem, The Laurentian Forest, Polar World and The Tropical Forest. Visitors walk through a man-made kingdom of trees, plants and animals, along a 500-metre path which is lined with interpretive plaques. The need to protect the environment is the major theme.

The mysteries of space are revealed at the **Montreal Planetarium**, a museum on Saint-Jacques Street which explains the forces that have fashioned the Universe. With the help of a huge Zeiss projector, images of the planet-studded heavens surround viewers, as commentators such as astrophysicist Hubert Reeves, interpret such complex topics as black holes and what causes collisions in space.

Montreal's Biodome is the only environmental museum of its kind. Visitors experience a tropical rainforest, the marine life of the St. Lawrence River and see thousands of plants and animals.

Although the beautiful and well-known Monarch butterfly is the emblem of the Montreal Insectarium, the two-floor exhibit displays many creepy, crawly critters like scorpions, maggots, locusts and tarantulas.

The Montreal Planetarium is an excellent place to learn about the night sky and an even better place to be entertained and have fun.

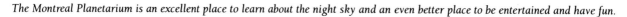

There are many tour companies which will take visitors out to experience Montreal by boat.

Ben's Deli is where the original, now famous, smoked-meat sandwich came from. The deli-restaurant was opened in 1908 by Ben and Fanny Kravitz and is still in the family today.

When exploring Montreal's attractions, visitors can enjoy eating out at the city's many restaurants. Among the more unusual places to eat is on a **Bateau Mouche**, one of the glass-topped sightseeing boats that ply the harbour. Leaving from the Vieux Port, the Bateau Mouche takes diners around Montreal's waterfront, sailing past Ile Saint-Hélène, Ile Notre-Dame, and under the Jacques Cartier and Victoria Bridges, affording the passengers spectacular views of Montreal's glittering skyline.

Ben's Deli & Restaurant is a Montreal landmark that has been in business since the beginning of the century. It was opened in 1908 by Ben Kravitz who started selling smoked meat sandwiches based on a recipe given to him by his Lithuanian mother. Smoked sandwiches and hearty, mostly Jewish, fare are still standards on the menu. The decor of the deli — vinyl-covered chairs, Formica counter tops and tiled floors — hasn't changed in 50 years, which is the main reason that Ben's is as much a tourist attraction as it is a place to eat.

Chinatown, which fans out in a north easterly direction from Montreal's Convention Centre, is crowded with interesting restaurants whose cuisine reflects a variety of Oriental origins. Immigrants to Montreal have come from Hong Kong, the People's Republic of China, Laos, Vietnam and Korea and many have set up businesses here.

Chinatown's inhabitants remain faithful to their traditions and have held together to resist molding with the modern part of the city that surrounds them.

Montreal's Chinatown is small, but interesting and colourful. It features many restaurants with the occasional church and grocery store.

The Chateau Dufresne, or the Musée des Arts décoratifs de Montréal, was built by the Dufresne brothers beginning in 1916. Once built, the brothers divided the house and then each filled his half with furniture, art and other items of the time — their goal was to live in style. Today, the house holds the largest Canadian collection of International-style 1940s and '50s furnishings.

The museum displays original furnishings and art as in the drawing room of Marius Dufresne.

(above) The drawing room of Oscar Dufresne.

(right) Montreal's Museum of Fine Arts is Canada's oldest museum. This original Greek Revival building, built in 1912, is made from Vermont marble. The modern annex was added in 1991, also made of marble, and is connected to the ancient Greek building by an underground tunnel that doubles as a museum gallery.

(right) The Jean-Noel Desmarais Pavilion, opened in 1991, is devoted to contemporary international and Canadian art after 1960. It also displays European paintings, sculpture and decorative arts that date from the Middle Ages to the 19th century.

MUSEUMS

Montreal's museums are rich repositories of the artwork and artifacts documenting the social, cultural and historical life of the city and of other parts of the world. The buildings in which they are housed are themselves often outstanding examples of their era. **Château Dufresne**, for instance, with its classical pillared entrance, is typical of the handsome beaux-art style popular in the mid-19th and early 20th centuries.

The château, whose interior is decorated with opulent Edwardian furnishings, was built between 1915 and 1918 by the wealthy Dufresne brothers, Oscar and Marius. It is now the home of the Montreal Museum of Decorative Arts. The lavishly decorated rooms, filled with furniture belonging to the Dufresnes, are a fitting setting for the objects and pieces of art displayed here.

The Montreal Museum of Fine Arts looks, at first glance, much like the Château Dufresne — or at least half of it does. Thanks to a recent addition, the art gallery actually comprises two buildings which face each other on Sherbrooke Street. The original Vermont marble

The Museum of Fine Arts has an extensive collection of art that equals more than 25,000 items.

(above right) Pastourelle; vallon Goujard (Seine et Oise) by Suzor-Coté.

(bottom right) La feerie by Fantin-Latour.

structure with its Ionic columns dates back to 1860 and the ultra-modern **Desmarais Pavilion**, designed by Israeli-born Moshe Safdie, opened in 1990.

A tunnel connects the two and visitors can walk freely from one building to the other. The benaiah Gibb Pavilion (the old part) highlights blockbuster art exhibitions from around the world. The modern Desmarais Pavilion, a light-filled space which gives great views over the city, has a fine art bookstore and a boutique which sells reproductions of museum exhibits.

The **Montreal Museum of Fine Arts** houses a permanent collection of engravings, drawings, sculpture and silverware. Paintings by well-known artists such as Québecois painter **Marc-Aurèle de Foy Suzor-Côté**, who studied his craft in France, are on display, as well as the works of Parisian painters such as **Henri Jean Théodore Fantin-Latour**, famous for his group portraits and his ability to portray light with an almost photographic realism.

The **Redpath Museum** which is on the campus of McGill University, was built in 1883 in the Greek Revival style by sugar baron Peter Redpath who donated the money for what was, at the time, Canada's first natural history museum. It has Canada's second-largest collection of Egyptian antiquities and the displays include such oddities as shrunken heads and a mummy in a glass case.

The **Point-à-Callière Museum of Archeology and History** looks like a stylized ship — an appropriate analogy, since it is "moored" on a wedge-shaped corner just across from the Vieux Port. Named for Louis-Hector de Callière, governor of Montreal from 1684 to 1698, whose house stood on the same spot, it encompasses three different exhibition areas — the modern Eperon building, a former customs house and a crypt dating back to the early days of settlement.

The museum marries the old with the new. Laser technology and holograms introduce visitors to figures from the past who relate Montreal's history in their own words. While you walk through the museum, you can see the excavated foundations of structures several centuries old. Collected at the museum are local artifacts spanning 300 years, found during archeological digs. Parts of Montreal's first Catholic cemetery have also been uncovered.

Marie-Marguerite d'Youville, who was educated by the Ursulines nuns of Quebec, founded the Sisters of Charity in 1737. Ten years later, she and four other women took over the bankrupt Montreal hospital and reorganized it into a hospice for orphans and aged men and women. The group evolved into the order of the Grey Nuns whose charitable work won them recognition throughout the French colony. The **Marguerite d'Youville Museum** on Saint-Mathieu Street is dedicated to her life and times.

(above) The Montreal Museum of Archeology and History can fittingly be found on the site where Montreal was established in 1642 — at Pointe-à-Callière. The museum is very popular because of its many impressive exhibits and displays.

The Marguerite d'Youville Museum tells the story of Marie-Marguerite d'Youville. Among other charitable acts she founded the Sisters of Charity in 1737.

(below) The Redpath Museum, a building dating from 1882, is actually a part of McGill University. It is most popular for its large collection of Egyptian antiques.

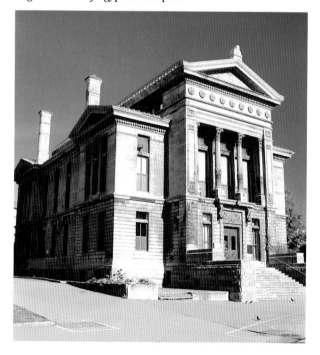

During the 30 years since its founding, the **Museum of Contemporary Art** has had several homes. Its latest building, which opened in 1992, is a stunning addition to Montreal's Place des Arts, the cultural centre of downtown. Designed by Montreal architect Gabriel Charbonneau, the light, airy structure, with its soaring walls, is an elegant exhibition space for the over 4,500 works of the modern artists and sculptors on display here — Jean Paul Riopelle, **Paul Émile Borduas**, Jack Bush and **Tony Cragg**, among others.

(left) The Museum of Contemporary Art is an impressive building in itself. It has eight large galleries which showcase a wide range of contemporary artists and their styles. The works of art are from local Quebec artists as well as artists from the rest of Canada and other parts of the world.

(below left) Sans titre (1942), by Paul-Emile Borduas.

(below right) Spiral (1983), by Tony Craig.

The **Château de Ramezay** Museum on rue Notre-Dame east, with its thick stone walls, tower and multi-paned windows, looks as if it has been transplanted from Normandy — not surprising, since it was designed by one of the leading architects in New France, Pierre Couturier, in 1705. He built it for Claude de Ramezay, governor of Montreal, who needed a new house to accommodate his wife and 16 children. Furnishings, artifacts and paintings highlight the history of the province of Quebec's early days.

Exhibits at the **McCord Museum of Canadian History**, near McGill University, also document Quebec's past but this establishment covers the rest of the country too. Its over 80,000 historical treasures include costumes, prints, paintings, books, textiles, costumes and an outstanding collection of Indian and Inuit artifacts.

The Chateau Ramezay, on rue Notre-Dame, was built by Claude de Ramezay in the early 1700s. This French Regime style building was home to the city's royal French governors for four decades. Then it was taken over by the British and used for their royal governors. In 1775, American rebels, invading Montreal, used the building as their headquarters. The chateau was used for a number of different purposes before becoming a museum in 1895.

The museum displays a painting of Jacques Cartier by a model of his boat "Emerillon".

The museum features the furnishings, tools, oil paintings and other items that depict the activities of the 18th century.

(far right) The David M. Stewart Museum, located on Ile Ste-Helene, was originally a fortified arsenal built by the British in 1822 for defense purposes. Today the volcanic-stone buildings contain the instruments, maps, artifacts and paraphernalia that were used in the days of Jacques Cartier.

(near right) This 17th-century armillary sphere from France is one of the many treasures that can be found at the David M. Stewart Museum.

Two other Montreal museums are worth noting — the **Stewart Museum** at the Fort and the **Canadian Centre for Architecture**, commonly called the CCA. The brainchild of Phyllis Lambert, a member of Montreal's wealthy Bronfman family (but an architect in her own right), the CCA, which is also a research centre, showcases modern architecture and urban landscapes. The Stewart Museum at the Fort, housed in the stone barracks on Ile Saint-Hélène, has a fascinating collection of old maps, firearms and navigational aids.

The McCord Museum of Canadian History features the costumes of European immigrants from as early as the 18th century.

The McCord Museum of Canadian History, a private museum, is forever changing to accommodate the many items in the collection of the museum founder, David Ross McCord (1844-1939), a lawyer, whose family immigrated to Quebec from Ireland in 1760.

(below) The entrance hall in the McCord Museum of Canadian History is impressive in itself and leads to many treasures from the past through the eyes of Canadian immigrants.

The Canadian Centre for Architecture, or the CCA building, fills a city block and is an impressive sight in itself. But inside, visitors wander through different moods and times evoked by the various designs and styles of the many exhibits.

The University of Montreal is the second-largest French speaking university in the world.

UNIVERSITIES

Montreal's educational life has come a long way since Marguerite de Bourgeoys, a French nun who established the city's first school (for girls) in 1658. There are now four universities —— **McGill**, **Concordia**, **Montreal** and the **University of Québec in Montreal** (UQAM).

The result of a legacy donated in the early 1800s by James McGill, a wealthy Scottish fur trader, McGill University has one of the most beautiful campuses of any Canadian college. Its 60 buildings sit on the side of a mountain which overlooks the city.

The University of Montreal is the second-largest French-speaking university in the world and its art deco pavilion with its central tower designed by architect Ernest Cormier, is a distinctive city landmark.

Open only since 1979, the University of Québec in Montreal, which is a base for some 40,000 students, is both new and old since it is, in part, the former St. James Cathedral, with its ornate Gothic facade.

McGill is one of the most prestigious universities in Canada.

(left) McGill is situated on the slope of Mount Royal. Many tourists take the free tour of the campus because of its beauty and location.

(below) Many visitors wander through the McGill gates to explore the beautiful campus.

The University of Québec in Montreal, or UQAM, is the newest university in Montreal but it keeps with the old theme of the city since its campus includes the former St. James Cathedral.

DOWNTOWN

Montreal is a city built for walking. The centre core is small and the downtown area, with its interesting architecture, handsome churches and green spaces dotted with trees and statues, makes it a pleasant place to stroll. When your feet get tired, a **Metro** (subway) station is never far away.

Montreal's downtown is rich with green grass and trees for all to enjoy.

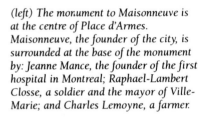

(left) The monument to Maisonneuve is at the centre of Place d'Armes. Maisonneuve, the founder of the city, is surrounded at the base of the monument by: Jeanne Mance, the founder of the first hospital in Montreal; Raphael-Lambert Closse, a soldier and the mayor of Ville-Marie; and Charles Lemoyne, a farmer.

(below) Montreal's Metro system is very popular with both tourists and residents. The underground system is speedy and affordable.

(above and right)This true replica, on a smaller scale, of St. Peter's Basilica in Rome was constructed from 1870 to 1894. Mary Queen of the World Cathedral is an impressive sight by day or night.

(left) The contrasting architecture in the city is complimenting and charming.

The main drag is **Ste-Catherine Street**, a colourful, noisy, east-west thoroughfare lined with restaurants, department stores, bars, clubs, fast-food outlets, cinemas, boutiques and souvenir shops. Street vendors sell a variety of goods, from flowers to imported jewelry. Ste. Catherine swings until the wee small hours and traffic jams at midnight are not at all uncommon.

Modern shopping malls accessible on foot or by Metro, add to the bewildering choice of consumer goods available to visitors. Shop until you drop (the city has over 7,000 stores) at Eaton's, Ogilvy, Place Bonaventure, Complexe Desjardins, Les Promenades del Cathédral or the elegant and pricey, **Cours Mont-Royal** on the east side of Peel Street.

Place Ville-Marie, with its 100 retail outlets, was the first building in Montreal's Underground city, a network of shops and restaurants designed to protect shoppers from the worst excesses of winter. In the 30-plus years since it first opened, the Underground City has expanded to include several hotels, thousands of offices, a couple of dozen movie theatres and more than 1,000 boutiques, connected by 18 kilometres of walkways.

Sherbrooke Street, which parallels Ste. Catherine, is the place to shop for designer clothes. Ritzy stores like Holt Renfrew rub shoulders with boutiques and art galleries housed in renovated, brick and greystone row homes. Sherbrooke has always been an elegant thoroughfare. In the 1700s, it was dominated by a grand, French-style château. A couple of stone towers from a fort on the same site, still stand. Two centuries later, the fur and lumber barons, each trying to outdo the other, built huge, rambling mansions. Sadly, some were pulled down in the development fever of the 1960s and '70s. But those remaining are marked with historic plaques.

Things happen on St. Catherine Street. It is definitely a favourite place to shop — both small shops and the big department stores can be found here. The street goes straight through Montreal's shopping and entertainment district.

(right and far right) Crescent Street is glamorous. It's a street where a lot of well dressed people with expensive cars can go to pricey boutiques and gourmet restaurants — but everyone is welcome.

Running south off Sherbrooke is **Crescent Street**, which, with its trendy bistros and sidewalk cafés, is a great spot for people watching. Montrealers love fashionable clothes and they aren't afraid to wear the most outrageous apparel.

Among the main characteristics of Montreal are its distinctive neighbourhoods. Each neighbourhood looks and feels like a separate village, as indeed many of them once were. Old Montreal, still the most distinctive of the "villages," used to be surrounded by a wall and when that was demolished in 1801, the city was free to develop and spread its tentacles into the communities that were then considered the suburbs.

The Latin Quarter, which encompasses **rue St-Denis** and rue Prince Arthur, is a student area and hangout for intellectuals and political types who debate long and hard in the many bistros and cafés. Prince Arthur is known for its reasonably priced eateries serving Greek and Italian food — where you can bring your own wine. No motorized traffic is allowed on the street and in the summer it turns into a giant stage for sidewalk performers — from flame eaters to artists who will sketch your portrait for a small fee.

Boulevard St-Laurent, or "the Main," as it is more commonly called (it was once the main south-north artery, hence its nickname), divides Montreal into east and west. A bustling, thoroughfare lined with fascinating food shops, it pulsates to the rhythm of its multi-ethnic population — Greeks, Eastern Europeans, Portuguese and South Americans. You'll hear a multitude of languages — from Yiddish to Romanian — spoken in the restaurants, food shops and corner stores which offer a cornucopia of exotic fare.

(left and above) Les Cours Mont-Royal, a modern restoration of the old Mount Royal Motel, is a popular and architecturally beautiful shopping complex.

(left) The typical charm of a flower vendor on St. Denis Street.

(right) Montreal's shopping streets include Sherbrooke, Crescent, St. Laurent, Laurier, St. Paul, Notre-Dame, Ste. Catherine and Peel. Many of Montreal's boutiques can be found on Crescent Street between Sherbrooke and Maisonneuve.

ENTERTAINMENT

It's not surprising that Montreal is known as the festival city of Canada. Montrealers are renowned for their "joie de vivre" and they'll use any occasion to stage a party. Music is also very much a part of every day life. In the summer, the Vieux Port, Old Montreal and several other venues around town, are alive with colour and sound.

Place des Arts, a complex of three buildings which overlooks a public square landscaped with fountains, is Montreal's principal centre for the performing arts, occupying a block between Boulevard Maisonneuve and Ste-Catherine West. **Les Grand Ballets Canadiens**, who have delighted audiences with their modern and classical dance for over 30 years, performs here regularly, as does the Montreal Symphony Orchestra (MSO), under conductor Charles Dutoit.

Musicians from around the world have performed with the MSO, considered to be one of the best symphony orchestras in the world. Place des Arts has played host to Frank Sinatra, composer Philip Glass and tenor Placido Domingo — just some of the leading luminaries who have appeared in the five theatres which make up the cultural centre.

Place des Arts is also one of the main venues for the **Montreal International Jazz Festival** held at the end of June and beginning of July. During the music fest, which headlines over 2,000 performers playing at 350 events around the city (many of the stages are set up outside), over one million music lovers flock to town to listen to jazz greats like Ornette Coleman, the Shirley Horn Trio and Montreal's own Oliver Jones, a pianist whose first teacher was the sister of Oscar Peterson, another renowned jazzman from Montreal.

This striking complex is the Place des Arts where a variety of talents are performed in the five halls it contains. Many famous and followed performers are seen here, including the Montreal Symphony Orchestra, who play in the Salle Wilfred-Pelletier Hall.

The Grands Ballets Canadiens is one company that performs at Place des Arts, in the heart of Montreal.

Montreal is one vast jazz festival at the end of June and beginning of July each year. The International Jazz Festival offers many free concerts daily as well as ticket concerts of famous jazz artists.

Juste Pour Rire/Just for Laughs, a bilingual comedy festival, started in a small way, in the early 80s, with a handful of stand-up comics. It has since become the premier comedy event in North America, attracting some 500 artists from as far away as France, New Zealand and India. Zany, hilarious performances are staged on and around rue St-Denis and the Vieux Port. During the past decade, legendary comics such as Milton Berle, Marcel Marceau, Steve Allen, Bob Newhart and Lily Tomlin have lent their talents to this unusual, annual event.

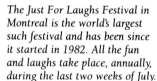

The Just For Laughs Festival in Montreal is the world's largest such festival and has been since it started in 1982. All the fun and laughs take place, annually, during the last two weeks of July.

(right) Montreal is famous for its annual Benson & Hedges International Fireworks Competition. La Ronde amusement park, on Ile Ste-Helene hosts the annual even in June and July.

The Montreal Canadiens are the favourite team of
many fans both in Montreal and across the country.

The city's National Hockey League team — the
Montreal Canadiens — have won 24 Stanley Cup
championships since 1929.

*Formula I drivers from around the world can be seen
racing on the Gilles-Villeneuve racetrack on Ile Notre-Dame during the annual Grand Prix of Canada event held in Montreal.*

Sports

October to mid-June is the hockey season in Montreal and during those months, visitors can enjoy the exciting and fastmoving games of the **Montreal Canadiens**. The Canadiens, in their signature red and white sweaters, zoom around the ice with death-defying speed and their superb players. Among them the fabled Maurice Richard after whom an arena is named — have always been among the best in North America. The Canadiens have won the Stanley Cup 24 times, more often than any other team in The National Hockey League.

The **Maurice Richard Arena** is part of the Olympic Park complex, built for the 1976 Summer Games. Centrepiece of the park is the impressive Olympic Stadium with its graceful, futuristic design — an oval of concrete dominated by a soaring, inclined tower — still looks very modern. A cable car hoists visitors 890 feet to the top, from which they get a bird's eye view over the city and the countryside beyond.

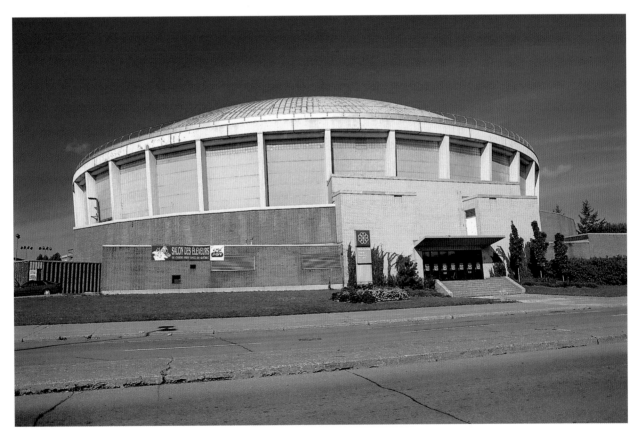

(above) Maurice Richard Arena is named for the Montreal Canadiens superstar who was known as "the Rocket". The Rocket scored 544 goals in his hockey career, from 1942 to 1959.

Less than an hour's drive from downtown Montreal are the Laurentian mountains and the Eastern Townships — "cottage country" for Montrealers. The Laurentians lie to the north of the city. The Eastern Townships, to the south.

The Laurentians, a mountainous region of lakes, forests and picturesque villages, has the highest concentration of ski resorts (over 20 at last count) in North America. The 968-metre **Mont Tremblant** ("trembling mountain" according to an Algonquin Indian description), is surrounded by a provincial park. Around Mont Tremblant (the name of a village as well as the mountain) are dozens of resort hotels, country inns and condominiums where vacationers can sail, swim, fish canoe or enjoy regional cuisine.

The Eastern Townships, which are called "Estrie" ("the Eastern Kingdom") in French, is also a popular ski centre. Four major peaks — Bromont, **Mount Sutton**, Mont Orford and Owl's Head — are situated within an hour's drive of one another.

Often compared to New England, Estrie is a rural enclave of rolling hills and farmland, dotted with country inns and picturesque villages, a landscape reminiscent of neighbouring Maine, Vermont and New Hampshire. Vacationers can hike, bike or drive along scenic backroads which offer panoramic views over the rustic countryside.

(above top) Beautiful Mont Tremblant, just 122 kilometres north of Montreal, is a popular place for vacationers all year round. Mont Tremblant is the highest peak in the Laurentians — it's no wonder it's a favourite place to ski and resort. Summer is just as busy in this area when people come to enjoy water sports, golfing, tennis and much more including relaxing and enjoying the scenery and surroundings.

(above middle) Mont Tremblant features an 18-hole championship golf course.

(left) Those interested in skiing around Montreal at places like Mount Sutton and others, can usually rely on good skiing snow from mid-December to mid-April.

(right) Montreal's modern Olympic Stadium seats 60,000 to 80,000 people. It is easily recognized by it's 626-foot inclined tower. The tower is used to operate the retractable Kevlar roof. Montrealers and people from all over the world visit the stadium to watch the Expos, concerts and tradeshows.

M ontreal is a city that leaves a lasting impact on the mind and in the heart. Vibrant, cosmopolitan and exotic, its bilingual, multicultural ambience, makes it one of the most unique communities in North America. There are shades of Europe here and of a historic past. Yet the overwhelming sense is of a city on the move, a metropolis of the future that will continue to leave its mark on the world until well into the next century.

Montreal has lost its title as Canada's centre of commerce but in terms of cultural ideas and institutions, it is the capital of the country. It's no coincidence that many of Canada's leading artists, fashion designers, musicians and film makers were born, or are based, in Montreal.

The city's chic ambience, trend-conscious population and enthusiastic audiences, open to the most avant-garde ideas, make it a fertile ground for creative minds.

This creative energy comes together in the festivals, museums and distinctive, lively, neighbourhoods that contribute to the pot-pourri of tourist attractions. But when things get too exciting and sensory overload takes over, Montrealers and visitors alike can escape to a quiet place. There are many enclaves of tranquility in the city, notably Mont Royal, its most distinctive landmark. Not far from Montreal, too, are regions of unparalleled beauty — from the Laurentian Mountains in the north, to the Eastern Townships in the south.

CONTENTS

Published and Distributed by

Irving Weisdorf & Co. Ltd.

2801 John Street,
Markham, Ontario   L3R 2Y8

Editor	Photo Research	Writer	Designer
Sandra Tonn	**Hilary Forrest**	**Helga Loverseed**	**Blair Kerrigan**

Photography by Larry Fisher

Irving Weisdorf & Co., Ltd.   11b, 15, 30c, 34a, 34b, 35, 39d, 42a, 48

Gerard Romany   31b, 49a, 49b, 51b, 53c, 62a, 62b

Michel Gagné   18, 19, 22, Back cover

Ignaz Fluri   8c, 51b, 51c, 62c, 62e, 62g, 62h, 63b, 63d

Muriel Brousseau Photo   59a, 59b, 59c, 59d

The following photos courtesy of:

AMARC
   Bob Burch   31a

Bank of Montreal   4c, 16b

Centre Canadien d'Architecture   43c, 43d, 43e

Club de Hockey Canadien, Inc.
   A. Pichette   58a, 58d

David Stewart Museum
   Giles Rivest   42d

Greater Montreal Convention and Tourist Bureau   55c, 56b, 57c
   Yano Philiptenenko   49c
   AMARC   30d

International Jazz Festival   55d, 62f, 63f

Just For Laughs   56a, 56c

Les Grands Ballets Canadiens
   David Cooper   55a
   Michael Slobddian   55b

McCord Museum of Canadian History
   Michel Brunelle   42b, 43a
   Marilyn Aitken   43b

McGill University   45e

Montreal Botanical Gardens and Insectarium   36c

Montreal Canadiens   58b

Planétarium de Montréal   36b

Mont Sutton   60c

Mont Tremblant Resort   60a, 60b, 63a

Musée d'Art Contemporain de Montréal
   Denis Farley   41b, 41c

Musée des Arts Décoratifs de Montréal
   Giles Rivest   38a, 38b, 38c

Musée des Beaux-Arts de Montréal   39a, 39b, 39c

Musée du Château Ramezay   42e, 42f

University of Quebec   45c, 45d

University of Montreal
   Bob Fisher   44